Heinemann Library
Des Plaines, Illinois

Jenny Ridgwell

© 1998 Reed Educational & Professional Publishing
Published by Heinemann Library,
an imprint of Reed Educational & Professional Publishing,
1350 East Touhy Avenue, Suite 240 West
Des Plaines, IL 60018

Designed by Celia Floyd
Illustrations by Barry Atkinson, pp. 9, 10, 12, 13, 20, 23, 24, 26, 28;
Oxford Illustrators, pp. 8, 17
Printed in Hong Kong / China

02 01 00 99 98
10 9 8 7 6 5 4 3 2 1

Library of Congress Cataloging-in-Publication Data

Ridgwell, Jenny.
    Bread / by Jenny Ridgwell.
       p.   cm. — (Food in focus)
    Includes bibliographical references and index.
    Summary: Examines bread as food around the world, discussing how
it is made, its history, ingredients, different flours, and health
aspects. Includes experiments and international recipes.
    ISBN 1-57572-654-8 (library binding)
    1. Bread—Juvenile literature.   [1. Bread.]   I. Title.
II. Series.
TX769.R56   1998
641.8'15—dc21   97-44112
                                                          CIP
                                                          AC

Acknowledgments
The Publishers would like to thank the following for permission to reproduce
photographs:
APV Baker, p. 7; Bridgeman Art Library, p. 6; Gareth Boden, pp. 4, 11, 14, 18, 21, 25,
27, 29; Robert Harding Picture Library, p. 5 (Robert Frerck); SIS Marketing, p. 19; Trip,
p. 15, Ask Images, p. 15 (bottom), H. Rogers

Cover photograph: Trevor Clifford

Every effort has been made to contact copyright holders of any material reproduced
in this book. Any omissions will be rectified in subsequent printings if notice is given
to the Publisher.

Some words are shown in bold, **like this**. You can find
out what they mean by looking in the Glossary.

Contents

Introduction

* *

What can bread be used for?

Bread is one of the most important foods eaten around the world. It is a valuable food for health, giving us energy, vitamins, minerals, and fiber to help keep our digestive systems healthy.

Bread comes in many shapes and sizes such as loaves, bagels, buns, muffins, and rolls. Because bread was often considered too precious to waste, leftover bread became the main ingredient of several famous recipes such as bread and butter pudding.

Some of the many varieties of bread around the world

What is it like?

The basic ingredients for breadmaking are flour and water. Wheat flour is the most popular as it contains **gluten**, a protein that helps form the structure and shape of the bread when it is baked or cooked by other methods. Flat breads, such as crispbreads, are made without **leavening agents**. These are substances such as **yeast** or baking powder, that are added to bread or cake mixtures to make them rise. Flat breads are called **unleavened breads**. **Leavened breads** are lighter than unleavened breads because they are made using leavening agents.

Other ingredients give flavor and color to bread recipes. Eggs, butter, sugar, spices, and dried fruits, like raisins and cherries, are used to make delicious sweet breads. Savory breads can be made from many ingredients, including cheese, olives, dried tomatoes, and herbs.

Bread is cooked in different ways.Although most breads are baked in an oven, they can also be cooked on metal plates or griddles and in a tandoor, a clay oven heated with hot charcoal.

Why and when do we eat it?

In many countries, bread is eaten not only with meals but as a popular snack food consumed throughout the day. Bread can be eaten on its own, spread with butter and other toppings—such as jam, marmalade, and peanut butter—or it can be made into toast. In European countries, such as France and Italy, crusty bread is eaten with meals. In Asia and South America, breads like chapatis and tortillas are used to dip into stews and soups. In the Middle East, flat pita breads are split open and stuffed with salad and meat.

Millions of sandwiches made from bread are eaten at lunchtime and are often sold ready-made from sandwich bars and supermarkets.

These people in Mexico are eating tortillas as a quick snack.

History of Breadmaking

Bread is one of the oldest foods in the world and was discovered over 5,000 years ago. Early breads were made from grass seeds ground into flour, mixed with water, and baked on a hot stone. The Ancient Egyptians were the first people to grind wheat and make it into bread. They were nicknamed the "bread eaters" because they ate so much of this food. At the time, bread was used as money. For instance, the workers who built the pyramids were paid in bread.

Flat, **unleavened bread** is made from flour and water and contains no **leavening agent**. However, if you leave a mixture of flour and water exposed to the air for a few days, **yeasts** in the air mix with the dough and produce bubbles of **carbon dioxide** gas. This type of "wild yeast" dough is known as **sourdough**. Today we add yeast to many bread recipes to make the bread rise.

A model of Egyptian servants making bread from around 2000 B.C.

Brown or white bread?

Through the ages most people ate coarse, whole-grain bread because white flour was expensive to make. In the nineteenth century, machinery improved the way wheat was ground. White flour became cheaper, allowing more people to buy white bread. Today, white bread is about as popular as wholewheat bread. Experts recommend that we eat more bread of every kind, particularly whole-grain bread, which is rich in nutrients and fiber.

For centuries bread was cooked mainly in the home in ovens or on griddles. In Roman times small bakeries began to bake bread for customers in villages and towns. Today, in many countries around the world, people still buy their bread fresh every day from the local bakery. In industrialized countries, however, most of the bread is now made in factory bakeries and sold in supermarkets. These stores may also have in-store bakeries producing range of freshly baked breads.

Modern bakeries produce thousands of loaves of bread a day.

Did you know?

- *The person who earns money for the family is often called the breadwinner.*
- *The Great Fire of London in 1666 was started by a baker and destroyed the baking industry in the city.*

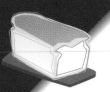

Growing Ingredients for Bread

Flour for breadmaking can be made ground from cereal grains, such as wheat, barley, oats, corn, and rye, or from dried roots, such as potato and cassava.

When a cereal grain or root grows well in an area, it becomes a **staple food** for the people who live there. A staple food, such as bread, forms a large part of the local diet.

Cereal grains

Wheat is the best cereal grain for breadmaking. It grows in temperate, cool areas of the world, including the U.S., Canada, Russia, and Australia. Today wheat bread is eaten in many countries around the world.

Corn originated from the Americas and was taken back to Europe by Christopher Columbus and other explorers. The crop became popular in Asia and Africa. Corn grows well in sunny climates, including the U.S., and is made into breads and breakfast cereals.

Rye is an important cereal grain in northern Europe and grows well in cool climates in poor soil. Rye breads are popular in Germany and Russia.

Oats grow in cool climates such as northern Europe. Traditional oatcakes come from Scotland.

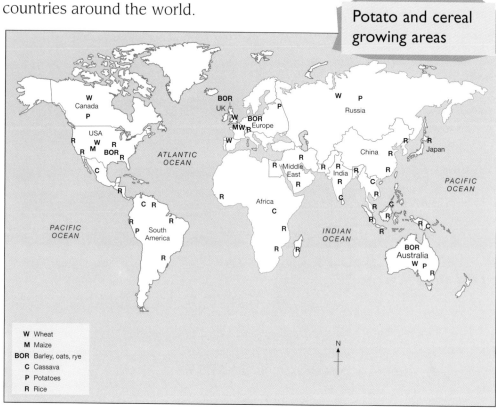

Potato and cereal growing areas

W	Wheat
M	Maize
BOR	Barley, oats, rye
C	Cassava
P	Potatoes
R	Rice

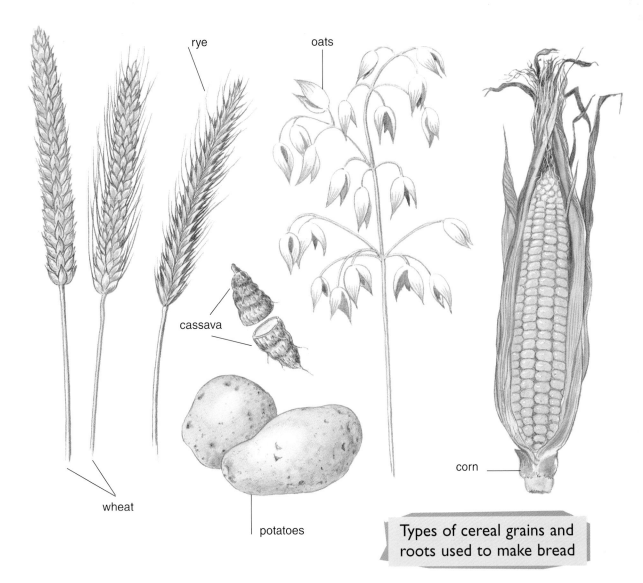

rye

oats

cassava

wheat

potatoes

corn

Types of cereal grains and roots used to make bread

Root crops

Although potatoes originally came from South America, today this important food crop is grown around the world. Potato flour can be used for breadmaking, but potatoes are usually eaten as vegetables.

Cassava is a root that also comes from South America and is an important food plant in the tropics. The roots are grated and made into a powder called meal, which can then be used for making bread.

People in rice-growing areas, such as parts of China, India, and Indonesia, eat boiled rice as their staple food instead of bread. As food is exported around the world, traditional rice-eating countries are eating more bread, while rice has become a popular part of the diet in countries that previously used bread as their staple food.

How is Bread Made?

Bread is usually made from wheat flour, water, and salt. **Unleavened bread** is flat and contains no **leavening agents** to make it rise. **Leavened bread** uses a leavening agent, such as **yeast,** to make the bread rise. Bread can be made in many different ways depending on the type of recipe.

Making leavened bread

What to do:

1. Mix flour, salt, and warm water with the yeast to make a soft dough.
2. **Knead** the dough to make it smooth and elastic and to stretch the **gluten** in the flour.
3. Shape the dough into a loaf and leave it in a warm place to **rise** and increase in size. Bubbles of gas are produced when yeast **ferments** and these bubbles help the bread to rise.
4. Bake the loaf in a hot oven. The bubbles of gas will expand in the heat and push up the bread dough. The dough sets and cooks until the outside is crisp and firm.

1   2

3   4

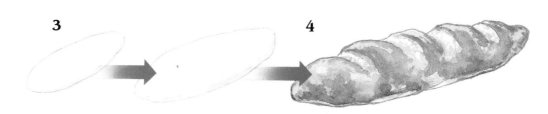

The ingredients

Yeast

Most bread recipes use compressed or active dry yeast. Yeast is a single-celled plant fungus used to make bread rise. Yeast needs food (from the flour), liquid (the water), and warmth in order to grow, ferment, and produce bubbles of carbon dioxide gas to make the dough rise.

Flour

Bread flour is best for breadmaking as it contains the most gluten. Gluten is a protein in flour and it helps to form the shape and framework of the bread. When bread dough is kneaded, the gluten is stretched, which improves the quality, texture, and structure of the baked bread.

Liquid

Water, or a liquid like milk, is used to mix the ingredients. The liquid should be warm to speed up the fermenting process. However, if the liquid is too hot, the yeast will be killed, and the bread will not rise.

Salt

Salt is an essential ingredient in bread. It provides flavor and helps to give bread a good shape and texture.

Many other ingredients can be added to bread to provide more flavor and texture. Delicious savory breads are made with crunchy seeds, nuts, cheese, herbs, and vegetables, such as dried tomatoes. Dried fruits, spices, and sugar are mixed with the bread dough to make sweet breads, such as teacakes and hot cross buns.

Bread is made from flour, liquid, yeast, and salt.

Flours for Breadmaking

Wheat flours

Wheat is the most popular cereal grain used for breadmaking. Wheat flour is made by **milling** or grinding clean grains of wheat.

The wheat grain is made up of three important parts:

- Endosperm makes up 85% of the grain and is used to make white flour.
- Bran makes up 12% of the grain. It is the outside husk and provides dietary fiber.
- Wheatgerm makes up 3% of the grain and contains vitamins and minerals.

Different sorts of flour use different proportions of the parts of the wheat grain.

White flour is made from the endosperm.

Bran flour is a mixture of white flour and bran.

Wheat-germ flour is white or brown flour with added wheatgerm.

Whole-grain flour is made from all parts of the wheat grain.

Stoneground flour is wholemeal flour ground in a traditional way between two stones.

A bread flour is best for breadmaking as the high protein content makes bread with a good structure and open texture. Bread flour comes from wheat grown with plenty of sunshine, so the grain develops a high level of protein.

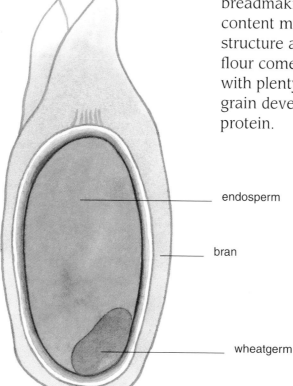

endosperm

bran

wheatgerm

The inside of a wheat grain

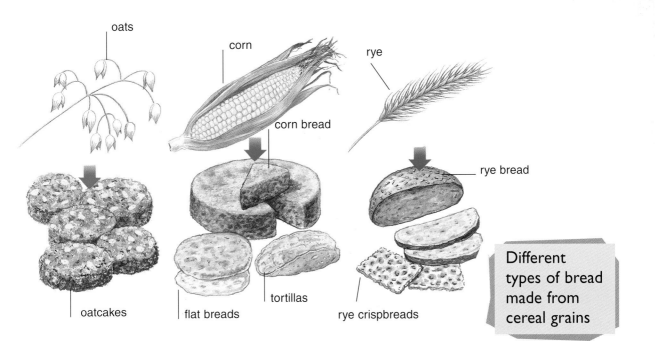

oats

corn

rye

corn bread

rye bread

oatcakes

flat breads

tortillas

rye crispbreads

Different types of bread made from cereal grains

Other flours

Other cereal grains and roots used to make bread include oats, corn, rye, barley, potato, and cassava. Each flour gives a special flavor, texture and color to the bread.

Oats are ground into oatmeal and made into flat oatcakes. Oatcakes are made by mixing oatmeal, water, salt, and fat into a dough, which is then pressed into thin biscuits and cooked in an oven. Oatcakes are popular in Scotland. To make a lightly risen bread, oatmeal needs to be mixed with wheat flour.

Corn can be ground into cornmeal and made into a soft, yellow cornbread, popular in the southern United States. In Mexico, corn flour is made into pancake-like tortillas.

Rye produces a darker flour than does wheat. The flour is made into rye crispbreads and dark brown bread that is firm to the touch. This bread is popular in northern Europe and Scandinavia.

Barley flour makes bread and baked products such as scones.

Potato flour is a fine white powder that can be used alone or mixed with wheat flour for bread.

Cassava flour is made from the tropical starchy root. The root is grated, dried, and made into bread, cakes, and wafers.

Some people like to eat **organic food** which is grown and processed without the use of pesticides and chemical fertilizers. Organic flour is milled from wheat grown and processed organically. Organic foods are often more expensive because the crops produce lower yields.

Bread Around the World

Thousands of varieties of breads are made around the world.

Flat breads include crispbreads from Scandinavia and Mexican tortillas. Tortillas are grilled on large, flat iron pans and eaten with spicy stews and snacks. In India, Pakistan, and Bangladesh flat breads are served at mealtimes.

Indian chapatis are made by rolling the dough into a disc shape and cooking it on a metal plate called a tawa. Parathas are heavier, layered breads, sometimes filled with vegetables. Nan bread is usually made with **yeast** and cooked in a tandoori oven.

Flat breads include pita and tortillas

Matza is an **unleavened bread** which is eaten by Jewish people at Passover. It represents the hurried departure of the Israelites from Egypt when people had no time to let the bread **rise.**

Bread can be shaped by cooking it in special pans to make loaves for slicing or it can be molded into shapes such as cottage loaves and French baguettes. The dough can also be twisted, braided, or decorated by cutting it with a cross or slashes.

Irish soda bread is made using baking soda instead of yeast as a leavening agent. Pumpernickel and rye bread, made from rye flour, are popular breads in northern Europe.

Hard dough bread comes from the Caribbean. The dough has sugar added to it and is made using a long rising process to make the bread firm and sweet.

Special occasions

Breads are made for special occasions such as festivals and feasts. Hot cross buns are small fruit buns with a cross on top and are eaten at Easter time. Greek Easter bread has colored, hard-boiled eggs baked into the loaf.

In Mexico, bread is made for the *Dia de Muertos* (the Day of the Dead), celebrated on November 2nd.

Challah bread is usually eaten on the Jewish Sabbath. This bread is braided and can be broken into pieces for serving.

Panettone is a Christmas bread from northern Italy which is made with candied fruit and raisins.

Harvest bread is made in Britain to celebrate the harvest in the autumn when the ripe cereal grains are gathered. Harvest bread is shaped like a traditional wheat sheaf, which represents the old way of stacking the wheat to dry in the fields.

Special bread is made for the Mexican Day of the Dead.

Harvest bread is made in the shape of a wheat sheaf.

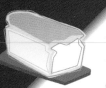

How is Sliced Bread Made?

Large commercial bakeries make most of the bread we eat today. These bakeries often run twenty-four hours a day, seven days a week to produce millions of perfectly baked loaves of bread.

The ingredients

The basic ingredients for bread baked on a large scale are flour, salt, **improver** (which speeds up the breadmaking process), **yeast,** and water. Many types of flour can be used, including white, whole wheat, and rye flours. Extra ingredients such as oats, and wheat germ can be added according to the chosen recipe.

Computer control

Bread baking in large bakeries is controlled by a complex computer system. The ingredients are precisely measured and the computer controls the baking process to make sure each batch of loaves has the same texture, taste, and weight.

Large bakeries can produce billions of perfectly baked loaves every week.

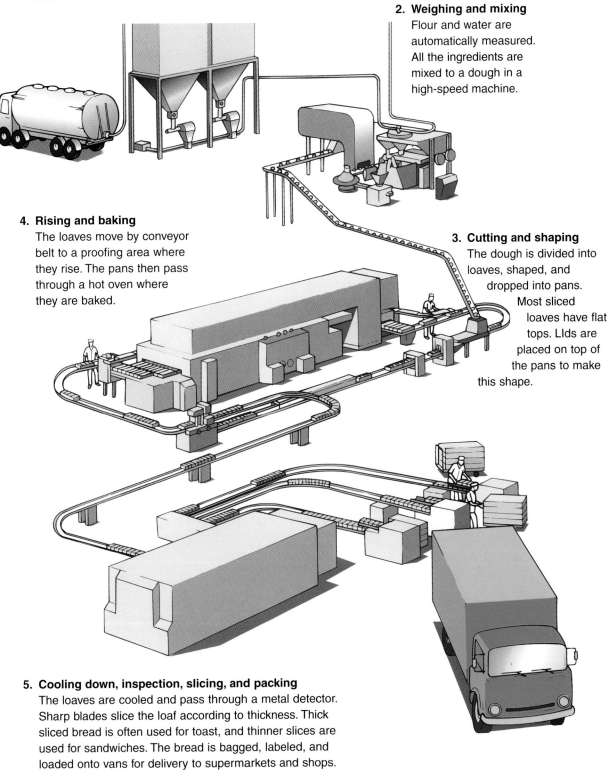

1. Delivery and storage
Flour arrives in the bakeries in tankers and is stored in silos before it is sifted.

2. Weighing and mixing
Flour and water are automatically measured. All the ingredients are mixed to a dough in a high-speed machine.

4. Rising and baking
The loaves move by conveyor belt to a proofing area where they rise. The pans then pass through a hot oven where they are baked.

3. Cutting and shaping
The dough is divided into loaves, shaped, and dropped into pans. Most sliced loaves have flat tops. Lids are placed on top of the pans to make this shape.

5. Cooling down, inspection, slicing, and packing
The loaves are cooled and pass through a metal detector. Sharp blades slice the loaf according to thickness. Thick sliced bread is often used for toast, and thinner slices are used for sandwiches. The bread is bagged, labeled, and loaded onto vans for delivery to supermarkets and shops.

Bread Today

Ways of buying and packing bread

In recent years, bread products and packaging have been designed to save time and to help keep bread fresh longer.

Gas packing extends the shelf life of packaged bread. The shelf life is the amount of time the product can be stored and still be safe to eat. The air inside the packaging is replaced with a mixture of **carbon dioxide** and nitrogen gas, which delays the growth of molds in bread. Gas packing is used for bagels, bread, partly baked breads, and pita bread.

Additives in bread

The additives used in food are strictly tested. Your choice of foods would be reduced if additives were not allowed. The additives in packaged bread are listed on the label. These may include vitamin C (ascorbic acid), which improves the texture of the bread, and emulsifying agents and preservatives that help the bread stay fresh longer and improve its shelf life.

Bread products can be packed with special gas packing to help them stay fresh longer.

Bread changes for diet and health

Some people have a condition known as celiac disease and are allergic to **gluten**, which is a protein found in wheat and other flours. Gluten-sensitive people can buy or make bread from gluten-free flours, which come from a variety of cereal grains, such as corn and rice.

Although we are encouraged to eat more fiber, many people like to eat white bread which contains little fiber.

If you like the taste of freshly baked bread, you can buy partly-baked bread and finish the cooking yourself. If you like homemade bread, a breadmaking machine is simple to use. Put all the ingredients into the machine and set the dials. The machine mixes, **kneads**, **proofs,** and cooks the dough in the one container. (Kneading is the process of pulling and stretching the dough to improve the texture of the baked bread. Proofing is the step in the breadmaking process when the bread dough is left in a warm place to rise.) When the loaf is baked, take it out of the machine, and let it cool. You have a loaf of bread.

An electric bread machine

Bread and Health

The food pyramid

Bread is an important food in a healthy diet. The **food pyramid** shows how to make healthy food choices. Our diet should contain a wide variety of different foods to provide the range of nutrients that we need.

The food pyramid suggests that we eat plenty of bread, cereal grains, rice, and pasta along with several servings of fruits and vegetables. These foods are shown in the lower section of the pyramid.

Foods from the top of the pyramid include fats, oils, and sugary foods. For better health we should eat less of these foods.

How healthy is bread?

Bread is a nutritious food. It provides us with energy, fiber, vitamins, and minerals that we need for our good health.

Over 50% of our energy intake should come from fiber-rich carbohydrate foods like bread. Nutrition experts suggest that we eat up to six slices of bread a day.

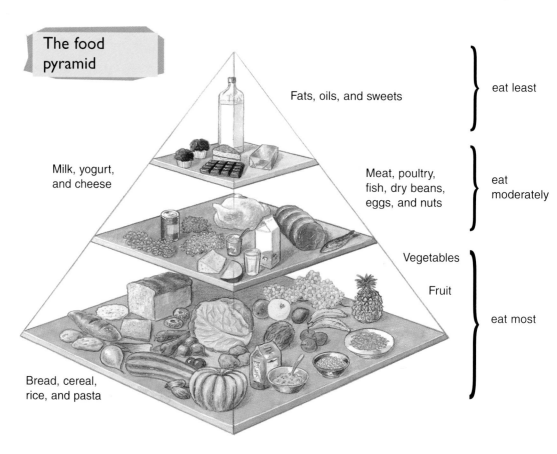

The food pyramid

Fats, oils, and sweets — eat least

Milk, yogurt, and cheese

Meat, poultry, fish, dry beans, eggs, and nuts — eat moderately

Vegetables

Fruit

eat most

Bread, cereal, rice, and pasta

Complex carbohydrates

Bread is a major source of **complex carbohydrate** in the form of starch. Because this is a long-lasting energy source, bread can be filling without providing too many **calories**.

Energy

The energy from bread, in the form of calories, comes mostly from carbohydrate. Bread is a low-fat food. It is the fat that you add, such as butter and spreads, that increases the calories.

We should eat six slices of bread a day as part of a healthy diet.

Fiber

Cereal grain products, including all types of bread, are good sources of fiber. Fiber is important to prevent constipation. Whole-grain and rye bread have more fiber than does white bread.

Protein

Bread provides protein, which is needed for growth, maintenance, and repair of the body.

Calcium and iron

Calcium is a mineral needed for strong bones and teeth. Iron is needed for healthy blood. Bread provides calcium and iron. Some brands of white breads are fortified with these minerals.

B vitamins

Cereal grain products such as bread are good sources of the B vitamins, which are needed to help nerves and muscles function.

Experiments with Yeast

Leavening agents are added to mixtures, such as bread and cakes, to make them rise. **Yeast** is a leavening agent often used in breadmaking. Yeast is a single-celled plant fungus whose cells are so small that they can be seen only under a microscope. Always wash your hands before and after handling yeast.

Yeast under the microscope

You will need:

- compressed and active dry yeast
- water
- 2 microscope slides
- a microscope

What to do:

1 Take some compressed yeast and mix it with a little water.
2 Smear some of this mixture onto a microscope slide.
3 Place the slide under the microscope and focus the lens so that you can see the yeast cells.
4 Repeat the experiment using active dry yeast.
5 Compare the shape and size of the compressed and active dry yeast cells as seen under the microscope.

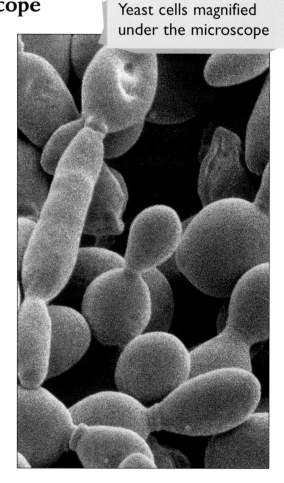

Yeast cells magnified under the microscope

When bread is made, the yeast grows and **ferments** giving off **carbon dioxide** gas and alcohol. The carbon dioxide gas expands during breadmaking and baking and pushes up the dough.

What does yeast need to grow and ferment?

You will need:

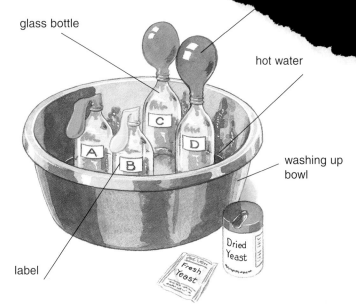

glass bottle

hot water

washing up bowl

label

Dried Yeast

Fresh Yeast

- compressed or active dry yeast
- teaspoon, tablespoon
- sugar
- 4 small glass bottles
- water
- 4 balloons to cover each bottle
- digital scales
- 4 labels
- tablespoon
- washing up bowl

What to do:

1 Label the bottles A, B, C and D.

2 Put $1/2$ teaspoon yeast (compressed or active dry) into each.

3 Add one tablespoonful (15 ml) of cold water to A.
Add one tablespoonful (15 ml) of warm water to B.
Add one tablespoonful (15 ml) of cold water and one teaspoonful (5 ml) sugar to C.
Add one tablespoonful (15 ml) of warm water and one teaspoonful (5 ml) sugar to D.

4 Put your finger over the end of each bottle and shake thoroughly. Cover the end of each with a balloon.

5 Stand all the bottles in a bowl of hot water for 20 minutes.

6 Watch what happens to each of the yeast mixtures and the balloons. Do any of the balloons expand? Which ones?

What should happen?

Yeast needs food (the sugar), liquid (the water), and warmth to grow and ferment. In experiment D, the yeast feeds on the sugar and grows in the warm water to produce carbon dioxide gas. When this gas is produced, the balloon expands. You may find the balloon on C expands because the mixture becomes warm from the water in the bowl. The balloons in experiments A and B will not expand because the yeast has no food so it cannot grow and produce carbon dioxide gas.

Try changing this experiment by adding salt or flour instead of sugar or by using boiling water.

cipe: Whole Wheat Bread Rolls

This bread roll recipe is based on a traditional European recipe that calls for fresh **yeast**. To speed things up active dry yeast has been used in this case. You can make these bread rolls into a variety of shapes—round rolls, small cottage loaves, braids, and twists. To make a loaf from this recipe, put the entire mixture into a bread pan and allow extra cooking time. Before you start ask an adult to help.

You will need:

Makes 8 rolls

Ingredients

- 3 1/3 cups (500 g) bread flour
- I teaspoon (5 ml) salt
- I package active dry yeast
- I tablespoon vegetable oil
- I 1/4 cups (300 ml) lukewarm water
- extra flour for kneading
- extra oil for brushing
- toppings—oats, flour, sesame seeds, or poppy seeds

Equipment

- scales (if you are weighing ingredients)
- pastry brush
- large mixing bowl
- teaspoon, tablespoon,
- wooden spoon
- measuring cup
- baking sheet
- plastic wrap
- oven mitts
- wire rack

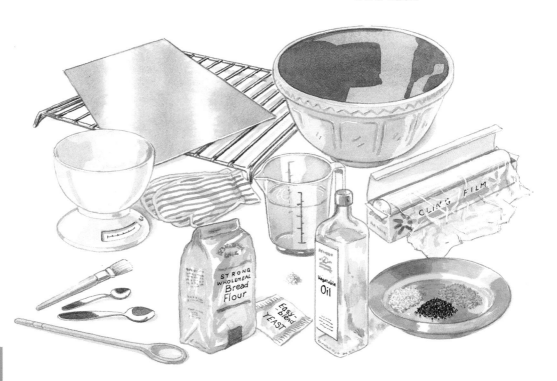

What to do:

1. Preheat the oven to 450°F (230°C). Brush the baking sheet with a little oil to prevent the bread rolls from sticking during baking.
2. Mix the flour, salt, and yeast in a bowl.
3. Using a wooden spoon gradually stir in the oil and lukewarm water until the mixture forms a soft but not sticky dough. You may not need to add all the water.
4. Place the dough onto a floured surface. Knead the dough by pushing and stretching it with your hands for 8 to10 minutes.
5. On a floured surface, roll the dough into a sausage shape. Divide the dough into eight equally sized pieces.
6. Roll each piece of dough into a smooth ball and place on a baking sheet.
7. Cover the bread rolls with plastic wrap you've brushed with oil.
8. Leave the rolls in a warm place to rise until they have doubled in size (one to two hours).
9. Remove the plastic wrap and sprinkle some flaked oats, flour, sesame seeds, or poppy seeds on the top of each roll.
10. Place the baking sheet on the top rack of the oven until the rolls are golden brown (about 15 minutes). Remove from the oven using oven mitts and cool on a wire rack.

These whole wheat rolls were dusted with flour before cooking.

Recipe: Soda Bread with Cheese and Herbs

This recipe is like a traditional Irish soda bread, with added cheese and herbs. You can eat soda bread with soup and salads or sliced for sandwiches. Baking soda is used as the **leavening agent** instead of **yeast**. You can change the flavor of the bread by adding other ingredients, such as dried fruit, candied cherries, and sugar. Before you start, ask an adult to help.

You will need:

Makes 1 loaf to serve 4 people.

Ingredients

- 1 1/3 cups (200 g) whole wheat bread flour
- 1/3 cup (50 g) plain white flour
- 2 tablespoons (20 g) rolled oats
- 1 teaspoon (5 ml) baking soda
- 1 teaspoon (5 ml) salt
- 1 3/4 oz (50 g) grated cheese
- 1/2 teaspoon mixed dried herbs
- 3/4 to 7/8 cup (170 to 200 ml) milk
- extra flour for kneading
- cooking oil

Equipment

- scales (if you are measuring ingredients)
- pastry brush
- large mixing bowl
- teaspoon
- wooden spoon
- measuring cup
- baking sheet
- knife
- oven mitts
- wire rack

What to do:

1 Preheat the oven to 400°F (200°C). Brush the baking sheet with a little oil to prevent the bread from sticking during baking.
2 Mix the flours, oats, baking soda, salt, cheese, and herbs in a bowl.
3 Gradually stir in enough milk to make a stiff dough.
4 Put the dough on a floured surface. Knead the dough for 2 minutes.
5 Shape into a large round loaf and place on the oiled baking sheet. Cut a deep cross in the top using a knife.
6 Bake in a hot oven for 30 minutes until the bottom of the loaf sounds hollow when tapped.
7 Remove the loaf from the oven using oven mitts and cool on a wire rack.

Soda bread

Recipe: Fruity Pizza

Pizzas were originally an ancient Roman breakfast food made from bread baked with cheese. Today pizzas are eaten in many parts of the world. They are made with a huge range of savory and sweet toppings. For this fruit pizza you can use fresh or canned pieces of fruit for the topping. Pizzas can be eaten as a snack or this fruity pizza may be served as a dessert. Before you start, ask an adult to help.

You will need:

Makes 2 pizzas to serve 4 people

Ingredients

- 1 1/2 cups (225 g) bread flour
- 1 teaspoon (5 ml) salt
- package active dry yeast
- 1/2 level teaspoon allspice or cinnamon
- 2 tablespoons (15 g) granulated sugar
- about 2/3 cup (150 ml) lukewarm milk
- extra flour for kneading
- cooking oil

Topping:
- 3 1/2 oz (100 g) soft white cheese such as Mascarpone
- 2 tablespoons (30 ml) honey
- fruit topping: slices of fruit such as banana, pineapple, cherries

Equipment

- scales (if you are measuring ingredients)
- pastry brush
- large mixing bowl
- small mixing bowl
- teaspoon, tablespoon, wooden spoon
- measuring cup
- rolling pin
- baking sheet
- oven mitts
- knife
- cutting board

What to do:

1. Preheat the oven to 450°F (230°C). Brush the baking sheet with a little oil to prevent the pizzas from sticking during baking.
2. Mix the flour, salt, yeast, allspice, and sugar in a bowl.
3. Using a wooden spoon, gradually stir in the lukewarm milk until the mixture forms a soft but not sticky dough. You may need to add more milk, depending upon the dryness of the mixture.
4. Place the dough on a floured surface. Knead the dough by pushing and stretching it with your hands for 8 to 10 minutes.
5. Using a rolling pin, roll the dough on a floured surface into two circles about 6 to 8 inches (15 to 20 cm) in diameter. Place on the baking sheet.
6. Mix the soft cheese with one tablespoon (15 ml) of honey. Spread this mixture on the two pizza bases.
7. Slice the fruit and place on the top of the pizzas. Spoon the remaining honey over the fruit.
8. Leave the pizzas in a warm place to rise until they have doubled in size.
9. Place the pizzas on the top rack of the oven and bake for about 15 minutes until the pizzas are firm underneath.
10. Remove from the oven using oven mitts.
11. Eat warm or cold with more fresh fruit or ice cream.

Fruity pizza

Glossary

calorie a unit used to measure the energy value of food

carbon dioxide the gas produced when yeast ferments. these gas bubbles help the bread to **rise**

complex carbohydrate a carbohydrate in the form of starch

ferment to cause a chemical change that takes place during breadmaking that produces carbon dixoide and alcohol and helps the bread to rise. The process is known as fermentation

food pyramid a system designed to help people make healthy food choices

gas packing changing the air in the package so that the food will keep longer

gluten a protein in flour that helps to form the bread framework, which is the structure or shape of the loaf or roll

improver a substance added to the bread dough during large scale manufacture to speed up the breadmaking process

kneading stretching and pressing the dough to improve the quality and texture of the baked bread

leavened bread bread made using a **leavening agent** such as yeast or baking soda

leavening agent a substance added to a baking mixture, such as a bread or cake, to help it rise

milling the process of grinding the cereal grain into flour

organic food food produced without the use of chemical pesticides and fertilizers

proof see **rise**

rise when bread dough is left in a warm place to allow for increase in size (also called **proofing**)

sourdough a dough that can be made using wild yeast

staple food a food, such as bread, that forms a large part of the diet

unleavened bread flat bread that does not use a **leavening agent** such as **yeast.** Unleavened breads include matza and chapatis.

yeast a single-celled fungus used to make bread rise

More Books to Read

Badt, Karin L. *Pass the Bread!* Danbury, CT: Children's Press, 1995.

Baskerville, Judith. *Bread.* Ada, OK: Garrett Educational Corporation, 1991.

Harbison, Elizabeth. *Loaves of Fun.* Chicago: Chicago Review Press, 1997.

Index